A railway journey can be fun.
The engine at the head of the train has a
number on its side. But have you ever noticed
that many engines have a name as well?
As the train speeds along the noise it makes
keeps changing, from a clicking noise to the
familiar 'diddle-de-dum diddle-de-dum' to a
steady roaring noise.
Alongside the track there are strange signposts,
such as, for instance, '1 in 150'.
And sometimes, as well as the ordinary whistle
signal, you can hear another sort—the very loud
bang of something called a detonator.
*Look at Railways* tells you everything you
want to know about trains.

Also in this series in Panther Books

Look at Castles *by Alfred Duggan*
Look at Theatres *by Ivor Brown*
Look at Zoos *by Gerald Durrell*
Look at Aircraft *by Philip Joubert*
Look at Stars *by Dr. H. C. King*
Look at Parliament *by Kenneth Robinson M.P.*
Look at Ponies *by Pamela Macgregor-Morris*

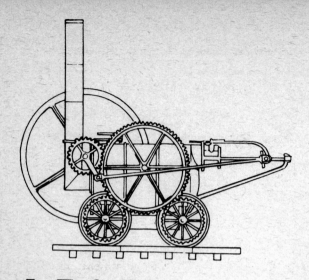

L. T. C. Rolt

# LOOK at RAILWAYS

Illustrated by John Young

A Panther Book

*A Panther Book*

First published in Great Britain by
Hamish Hamilton Limited 1959
Reprinted 1960, 1963, 1967
Panther revised edition published 1969
Copyright © L.T.C. Rolt 1969
Illustrations copyright © John Young 1969

Printed in England by
C. Nicholls & Company Ltd.,
The Philips Park Press, Manchester,
and published by Panther Books,
3 Upper James Street, London, W.1

# Contents

# How railways began

THE idea of a rail way is a very old one. Hundreds of years ago, long before there were any smooth roads, men discovered that it was very much easier to push or to pull a loaded wagon along on rails than over soft or uneven ground. These rails were long strips of wood which they laid down for the wagon wheels to run upon.

To keep these wooden rails the right distance apart they nailed them to wooden cross pieces which they called 'sleepers'. So that the wagons would stay on the rails the wooden wheels were specially made with raised rims called 'flanges' on the inside.

The earliest of these wooden railways were very small ones and were laid in mines so that men could push the little trucks of coal or minerals more easily through the underground tunnels.

Later, bigger and longer railways were laid down which ran from these mines to the sea or to the bank of a big river where the contents of the wagons could be tipped into boats. On these larger railways trains of wagons were coupled together and hauled along by horses. Some of the first of these wooden railways, or wagonways as they were sometimes called, were laid down near Newcastle between the coal mines there and the River Tyne.

The trouble with the old wooden rails was that they soon wore out or got broken, so about 200 years ago men started to make rails out of cast iron instead. These cast iron rails were of two kinds. One kind were called edge rails. They were rather like the old wooden rails and the wagons which ran on them had the same kind of flanged wheels. The other kind were called plate rails or 'tram-plates'. These were flat plates, each about three feet long, on which the wheels ran and each plate had an upright edge or flange on the inside to keep the

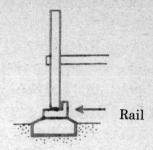

Rail

wheels in their place.

Because the flange was on the rails, the rims of the wagon wheels could be flat. The advantage of this was that such wagons could be used on the road as well as on the railway. In fact, ordinary carts could use a plateway of this kind if the wheels were the right distance apart.

If you measure the distance between the wheels of an ordinary farm cart you will find it is about 4 ft. 8 ins., and it was for this reason that many of these plateways were laid to this width, or gauge as it is called. You will only find these old plate rails in museums today, yet we still call the men who look after the tracks of our railways 'platelayers'.

Instead of wooden sleepers, the cast iron rails were often fastened down to big square blocks of stone. Where edge rails were used they were mounted on the stone blocks in special cast iron brackets called 'chairs'. In places where these early railways once ran you can sometimes find the old stone blocks built into walls or buildings.

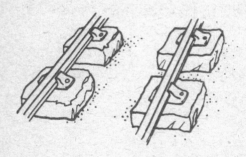

They are easy to recognise because each block had two holes bored in it. These holes once had wooden plugs in them and they were used to fasten down the chairs or the tram-plates.

The first railways of this kind were all private ones. That is to say, they were built by colliery or quarry owners for their own use. But in 1801 the British Parliament allowed the building of the Surrey Iron Railway. Anyone could haul their goods along this railway so long as they paid the company who owned it money for doing so, and it was therefore the first 'public' railway in the world. Nine miles long, it ran from Wandsworth to Croydon and it had two tracks.

# The first railway engines

WHILE the owners of coal mines were using railways to take their coal away to the nearest river, canal or seaport, they were also using steam engines to pump the water out of their mines and, later, to wind up the coal from the pit. The first engine ever used for pumping water from a mine was designed and built by a Cornish engineer named Thomas Newcomen.

This first engine was greatly improved upon by the famous engineer James Watt. Watt's engine was a wonderful machine in its day, but he intended it only for pumping or for driving machinery. It could not possibly be used to move itself along a railway and haul wagons behind it because it was much too heavy, too big and could not run fast enough.

The first man to make a steam engine small enough and light enough

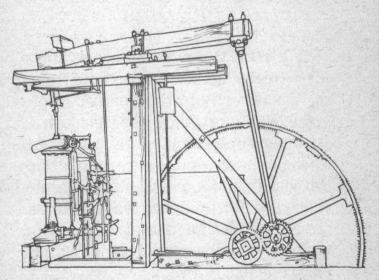

and at the same time strong enough to be used on a railway was another great Cornish engineer named

Richard Trevithick. He did this by using steam at a much higher pressure than James Watt did. Watt said that Trevithick's machine was very dangerous and that the boiler would be sure to burst, but Trevithick took no notice and went on experimenting with his 'high pressure engine' as he called it.

He adapted one of these engines to run on a railway, and in February 1804, he tried it out for the first time on a plate tramway in South Wales. This tramway ran for nearly ten miles from the Pen-y-Daren Ironworks to a wharf on the nearest canal. The owner of this ironworks, whose name was Samuel Homfray, bet a friend of his 500 guineas that Trevithick's new engine would be able to haul ten tons of iron from one end of the tramway to the other. To everyone's amazement, the engine did this and so Homfray won his bet. This was the first steam engine in the world to haul a load

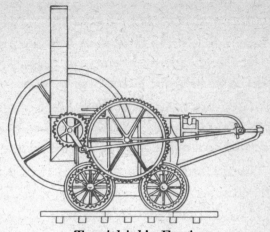

*Trevithick's Engine*

along a railway line.

To our eyes, this first engine of Trevithick's looks very odd indeed. It had only one cylinder, a huge flywheel and several big cog wheels to take the drive to the wheels. All the same, it worked. Its big fault was that although it was so much smaller and lighter than any steam engine which had been built before, it was still much too heavy for the tramway on which it was set to work.

Cast iron is a very brittle metal. It

will break like glass if you hit it hard enough. Trevithick's engine had no springs and as it bumped along the tramway, which was not as smooth and level as modern railways are, it smashed so many of the cast iron tram-plates that its use had to be stopped.

For some years after this nothing more was done and the railways went on using horses. Then the hay and chaff which the horses ate became very much more expensive because of the war England was fighting against Napoleon in France. This made the colliery owners of Tyneside think again about whether they could not use instead an 'iron horse' which would eat the coal which they produced themselves. Between 1812 and 1815 several clever engineers tried to give the colliery owners what they wanted, but it was a very difficult thing to do.

These engineers realised that a

'travelling engine', as they called it, had to be quite heavy. If it was not, there would not be enough weight on the wheels to make them grip on the smooth rails. Instead they would slip and spin round and the engine would never pull a heavy load. But a heavy engine would break the rails as Trevithick's had done. They had to think of some way of making a lighter engine pull a heavy load.

One of these early engineers, William Chapman, made an engine which pulled itself along on a rope; another, William Brunton, built what he called a 'walking engine' which pushed itself along on two feet.

More successful than these two were John Blenkinsop and Matthew Murray of Leeds. Instead of driving the carrying wheels, the two cylinders of their engine were connected to a single large cog wheel on one side. This wheel ran in a series of cogs which were cast on one side of one of the rails along the whole length of the line. In this way the engine and the railway were geared together and the little engine could pull as much as 90 tons.

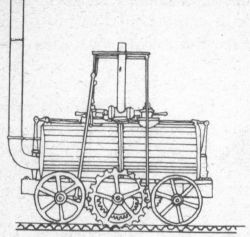

*The Blenkinsop Rack Engine*

This was called the rack-rail principle and it is still used today on lines which climb very steep hills, such as the Snowdon Mountain Railway in North Wales. The Blenkinsop rack engine was the first to do really 'useful' work. It ran for many years on the Middleton Colliery Railway, near

Leeds.

Near Newcastle there were two men who still believed that a useful railway engine could be built using smooth wheels and smooth rails in spite of the weight difficulty. One of them was named William Hedley. He designed

*Hedley's 'Puffing Billy'*

a famous engine which became known as 'Puffing Billy' and ran on the Wylam Colliery Plateway.

The second man was the mechanic

or 'engine wright' at Killingworth colliery only a few miles from Wylam. His name was George Stephenson and he built his first engine for the Killingworth Railway in 1814.

It was called the 'Blucher'. It was of a much simpler design than 'Puffing Billy', being very like Blenkinsop's engine but without the cog wheel drive. The Killingworth Railway was laid with cast iron edge rails of Stephenson's own improved design. This means that the 'Blucher' was the first engine to drive itself along on smooth flanged wheels just as engines do today.

# *George Stephenson*

**M**ANY people think that George Stephenson invented railways and railway engines. Now that you have read the last two chapters you know that this is not true. Yet George Sephenson and his only son Robert became famous while many of the other engineers we have talked about were forgotten. The real reason for this is that George Stephenson was the first man to look into the future and realise what the railway engine might become.

While the other engineers thought of it only as a substitute for horses on the short colliery lines, lumbering to and fro with loads of coal at a walking pace, Stephenson was sure the railway engine could soon be improved so much that it would be able to haul long trains carrying passengers as well as goods right across the country at high speed.

The engines which George Stephenson built for the Killingworth Railway went so well that he was asked to build more for other colliery lines in the neighbourhood. He was also asked to improve these lines by laying down his patent cast iron rails. Then, in 1821, he got his first big chance when the Stockton & Darlington Railway Company asked him to be their engineer.

The Stockton & Darlington Railway was planned to carry coal from collieries near Bishop Auckland in County Durham to a wharf on the

River Wear at Stockton. But it was a much bolder plan than the earlier colliery lines we have spoken about so far. It was twenty-five miles long, it served the town of Darlington on its way, and, like the Surrey Iron Railway which we mentioned in the first chapter, it was built as a 'public' railway under an Act of Parliament.

The leader of the little band of men in Darlington and Stockton who were determined to build this railway was named Edward Pease. He has often been called 'the Father of Railways' because, like George Stephenson, he was able to look ahead. At first Pease and his friends had intended using horses to pull the wagons on their new railway, but George Stephenson persuaded them to use his engines. In this way the Stockton & Darlington became the first 'public' railway in the world to use steam engines.

George Stephenson was starting to build this new railway in Durham when an engineer named John Birkenshaw made a very important invention. He worked at an ironworks at Bedlington near Morpeth in Northumberland. There he found a way of making rails out of wrought iron by passing bars of very hot metal through special rollers.

Now wrought iron is much stronger than cast iron. It is not brittle. If you hit it hard enough it might bend, but it would not snap like a cast iron rail. Because they broke so easily, the old cast iron rails could only be made in lengths of three feet. You can imagine then what an enormous number of rail joints there were and how the first railway engines must have jolted and bumped continually as they ran over these joints.

It was really hopeless for George Stephenson to think of making better and faster engines unless someone could think of a better and smoother kind of railway for them to run on.

This is what John Birkenshaw did. His stronger wrought iron rails were each 15 feet long so that there were far fewer joints.

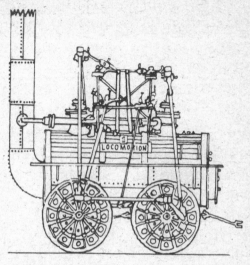

*Stephenson's 'Locomotion'*

George Stephenson knew that Birkenshaw's rails were far better than his and so he used them on the Stockton & Darlington Railway.

The Stockton & Darlington Railway was finished in September 1825, and

George Stephenson himself drove his new engine named 'Locomotion' which hauled the first train. This train was packed with people sitting in empty coal wagons. They must have had a very uncomfortable ride because these wagons had no springs, but nobody minded that. They were much too excited. For people whose only way of travelling was by horseback, or horse-drawn coaches or carts along rough roads it was a strange and wonderful experience which none of them ever forgot.

You can still see the famous engine 'Locomotion' if you travel by rail to the north of England by what is called the east coast route. The engine stands on the platform at Darlington station with another old Stockton & Darlington engine named 'Derwent' to keep her company.

Passengers were carried regularly on the Stockton & Darlington Railway from the beginning. But for some years the passenger carriages, which looked just like the old road coaches, were pulled by horses. Stephenson's engines, the 'Locomotion' and her sisters 'Hope', 'Black Diamond' and 'Diligence', could still only go very slowly. They were used for pulling the coal trains.

# The Liverpool & Manchester railway

A FEW months before the Stockton & Darlington Railway was finished, a new company was formed in Liverpool to make a railway from that city to Manchester, and George Stephenson was asked to build it. A lot of people tried to stop this railway being built. Some of them were big landowners who did not want the railway to come through their fields or parks; others owned canals and were afraid a new railway would take away their trade and ruin them. They said the railway was a mad, impossible idea and a great waste of money, but in spite of this the government eventually gave the company permission to build it.

It was a far more difficult line to make than the Stockton & Darlington. There was a long tunnel to be dug under part of Liverpool. Deep cuttings had to be driven through rock at a place called Olive Mount. A big stone viaduct had to be built to carry the railway over the valley of the Sankey brook.

Worst of all, the lines had to be carried across Chat Moss, a great bog so soft that men had to tie boards to their boots to prevent themselves sinking into it. Many engineers said it would be quite impossible to build a railway across such a bog, but George Stephenson did it. He sank thousands of bundles of brushwood in the bog until they formed a kind of raft on which the ballast, sleepers and rails could be laid.

From the beginning the company intended to carry passengers as well as goods on their new railway, but for a long time they could not make up their minds how the trains should be hauled along.

George Stephenson, of course, wanted them to use his steam engines, but although some of his employers went to see his engines working on the Stockton & Darlington line they doubted whether they would be fast or reliable enough to pull trains of passengers between Liverpool and Manchester. Some wanted to use horses. Others wanted to build a whole lot of stationary steam engines beside the line, spaced out in such a way that they could pull the trains from one to another by means of ropes.

This idea of pulling trains along with ropes may sound very silly now, but at that time many clever engineers thought it was the best plan and George Sephenson found it very hard to persuade the company to give his engines a fair trial. They eventually agreed to hold a competition for the best railway engine. This was to be held on a level part of their railway at Rainhill, near Liverpool, which had just been finished and they offered a prize of £500 for the winner.

Of course George Stephenson determined to win this prize. By this time he had started a factory in Newcastle to make steam engines and this was being run by his son, Robert Stephenson. While George went on building the railway, Robert started to make a new railway engine which would be much better than any engine made before.

The big trouble with all the engines which the Stephensons and other engineers had built so far was that the boilers could not make enough steam. So long as the engines went very slowly and did not have to run far without stopping this did not matter very much. But if an engineman tried to run too far or too fast, his engine used up more steam than the boiler could make. He would then have to stop, stoke up the fire and wait, just as your mother has to wait for her kettle to boil on the stove.

In the competition at Rainhill the engines would have to run up and down the line dragging a load of stone until they had covered 60 miles, which was equal to a journey from Liverpool to Manchester and back. The time would be taken for this journey and the engines would only be allowed to make one long stop when they had covered half the distance. Obviously an engine which could do this must have a much better boiler which could produce a lot more steam.

The two Stephensons knew this and so they made for their prize engine, which they called the 'Rocket', a new

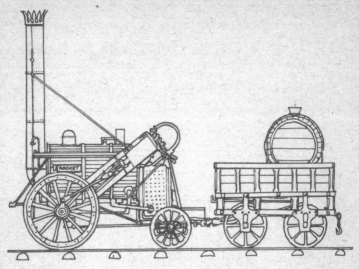

*Stephenson's 'Rocket'*

kind of boiler which was very much
the same as those used on steam railway engines today. The fire was put in
a box which had water all round it.
Before it was allowed to escape up the
chimney the heat from this fire was
taken through a lot of small pipes
which were also surrounded by water.
This meant that there was such a lot
of very hot metal touching the water

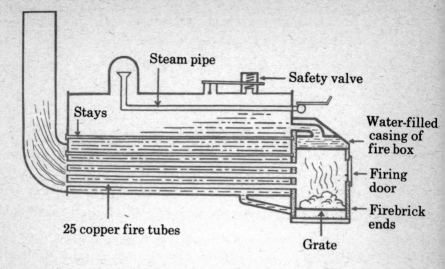

Steam pipe

Safety valve

Stays

Water-filled casing of fire box

Firing door

Firebrick ends

25 copper fire tubes

Grate

in the boiler that it boiled very quickly and very fiercely, giving off lots of steam.

Thousands of people came to Rainhill to watch the first competition between machines ever held. The two most dangerous rivals of the 'Rocket' were the 'Novelty', built by Braithwaite and Erikson of London, and the 'Sans Pareil' made by Timothy Hackworth, who was in charge of the engines on the Stockton & Darlington Railway. The 'Novelty' was easily the favourite with the crowd. It looked very smart in its bright blue paint and was the first engine to run. It went up and down the line by itself at a speed which amazed everybody, but it had little power. When it was coupled up to the test train it very soon failed.

The 'Sans Pareil' did better, but it burnt an enormous amount of fuel and had not finished its 60-mile test run before the pump which supplied the boiler with water went wrong. Driven by George Stephenson himself, the 'Rocket' was the only engine to complete the course and it therefore won the £500 prize. The 'Rocket' did more than meet all the conditions set by the judges of the trial, it improved upon them. Before the trial began, people had said it looked clumsy compared with the 'Novelty', but they did not understand the secret of its boiler or know that it was in fact much more soundly built than its rivals.

This great triumph for the Stephensons was to decide the future of railways. There was no more talk of horses or rope haulage on the Liverpool & Manchester Railway. The line was opened with great ceremony in

*Stephenson's 'Planet'*

September 1830. The Prime Minister, the Duke of Wellington, rode in a special state coach behind the latest Stephenson engine, the 'Northum-

37

brian', driven by George Stephenson. Next day the regular service of passenger trains between the two cities began. They have gone on run-

ning right up to the present day, for
this was the true beginning of the age
of railways as we know them.

The Stephensons very soon improved upon the 'Rocket'. Only a few weeks after the Liverpool & Manchester Railway was opened they sent to the line from Newcastle a new engine named the 'Planet'. This looked much simpler and neater than the earlier engines because all its parts were arranged in the same way that railway engines are built today.

# Railways everywhere

NOW men had learnt how to build railway engines like the 'Planet', which could travel fast over long distances without breaking down or running short of steam. They also knew how to make longer and stronger rails for such engines to run on. There was no longer any reason why railways could not be built all over the country.

Big landowners and the owners of canals or stage coaches still fought

against railways, but they were all
beaten. Thousands of miles of railways were made, not only in Britain
but all over the world. Big new
factories were built and great towns
grew round them, because for the first
time in history large numbers of
people and hundreds of tons of goods

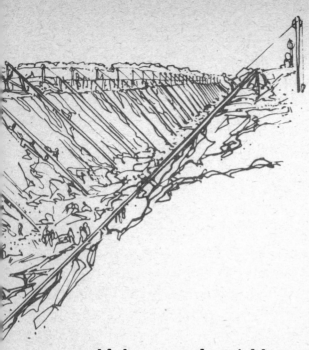

could be moved quickly and easily from place to place.

The first great main line of railway in England ran from the Liverpool & Manchester Railway through Birmingham to London. The part north of Birmingham was called the Grand Junction Railway and was built by an engineer named Joseph Locke who had been trained by George Stephenson. The southern half of this long line, the London & Birmingham Railway, ended at Euston Station in London and was built by Robert Stephenson.

Robert Stephenson had no machines to help him when he built this railway. Everything had to be done by the railway 'navvies' as they were called, using picks, shovels and wheelbarrows. The only help they had was from horses which drew wagons of earth along temporary railways or helped to pull heavy barrows up steep slopes.

Think of this next time you go on a railway journey and your train crosses a high embankment and viaduct over some river valley or runs into a deep cutting and from this into the darkness of a long tunnel.

The gauge of the Killingworth Colliery Railway where George Stephenson's first engine ran was 4 ft. $8\frac{1}{2}$ ins. He made all the other railways which he built the same width, and so did Joseph Locke and Robert Stephenson when they built the first long line to London.

But before they had finished it another great engineer began to make a railway called the Great Western from London to Bristol. He was the son of an engineer who had made the first tunnel under the Thames and his name was Isambard Kingdom Brunel.

Brunel did not see why the width between the rails on a great railway such as he was building should be the same as that of an old colliery line in the north. He thought that if the width was increased, bigger and more powerful engines could be built. He also thought that the trains would run much more steadily and could therefore safely go much faster. The passenger carriages could be made wider and more comfortable too.

So Brunel laid the rails on his Great

Western Railway seven feet apart and this was known as the 'broad gauge', while the width used by the Stephensons and other engineers was called the 'narrow gauge'.

Brunel's idea was a great success. The trains on his Great Western Railway were the first expresses in the world and could easily do sixty miles an hour at a time when the best trains on the narrow gauge could only manage half that speed.

But as more and more railways were opened, people began to realise how very awkward it was to have two different gauges. Wherever the two kinds of railway met, all the passengers had to change trains and all the goods had to be unloaded from one wagon into another. There was so much rivalry between the broad and the narrow lines that railwaymen speak of this time as the 'Battle of the Gauges'.

In spite of the success of his idea,

Brunel lost the battle for his broad gauge simply because the narrow gauge engineers had built so many more miles of railway than he had. It was very much easier and cheaper to make his railway narrower than it would have been to widen so many more miles of narrow gauge line.

In some places where it is very hilly, or where there are no big towns to make it worth the cost of making a big railway, little lines using a very narrow gauge were built. Miniature railways like the Romney, Hythe & Dymchurch have been built to a gauge of only fifteen inches, but the smallest gauge used on a real public railway is two feet. The first two-foot gauge railway in the world to haul its trains with steam engines (in 1863) was the Festiniog Railway in North Wales. The 2 ft. 3 ins. gauge Talyllyn Railway, also in Wales, started two years later. Both these little railways are still working.

If you have ever been to North Wales for a holiday you will know that it is full of mountains and that there are no big towns.

It was therefore many years before any passenger-carrying railways were built there. The first to come was Robert Stephenson's splendid railway to Holyhead which follows the north coast of Wales, and crosses the Menai Straits to Anglesey by a huge bridge, the first really big iron railway bridge

ever built.

This railway was finished in 1850, but its real object was to make a route from London to Ireland, using steam-boats between Holyhead and Dublin. It was another fifteen years or more before the people in the wild and mountainous parts of Wales and northern Scotland were served by rail-ways. By that time England had been covered with railway lines, stretching out in every direction from London and linking nearly every town in the country together. All these thousands of miles of railways were made in the fifty years since George Stephenson had built his first railway engine.

Our railway system was built by very many small companies, but gradually these joined together and formed bigger ones.

Then, after the First World War all these railways were grouped together to make four big companies, the London Midland & Scottish Railway, the London & North Eastern Railway, the Great Western Railway and the Southern Railway. A second big change came about after the last war when these four big companies were taken over by the State—or 'nationalised' as we call it. They are now divided into five regions known as London Midland, Eastern, Western, Southern and Scottish which are controlled from a single headquarters in London called the Railways Board.

Because of competition from road transport, many country branch lines and cross-country lines have been closed down. At the same time much has been done to bring up to date the

Railway Map of Great Britain in 1841

Glasgow
Kilmarnock
Ayr
Edinburgh
Carlisle Newcastle Shields
Sunderland
Durham
Darlington Stockton
Whitby
Pickering
Lancaster
Fleetwood York
Preston Leeds Hull
Wakefield
Liverpool Rotherham
Manchester Sheffield
Chester
Crewe
Derby Nottingham
Stafford
Leicester
Birmingham
Coventry
Stratford on Avon
Colchester
Llandeilofawr Stortford
Merthyr Gloucester Cheltenham Chelmsford
Tydvil
Llanelly London
Cardiff Whitstable
Bristol Reading Canterbury
Bath Dover
Bridgewater
Winchester
Southampton Brighton
Wadebridge
Bodmin

0 10 20 30 40 50 60
Miles

51

main lines which connect London with cities like Southampton, Bristol, Birmingham, Liverpool, Manchester and Glasgow. This has made possible much faster train services on such 'inter-city' routes.

# Carriages old & new

SO far we have said quite a lot about early railway engines but very little about the carriages they pulled. The first passenger trains looked very strange indeed. There were three classes of carriage instead of the two we have today.

The first class carriages looked very like the stage coaches of the roads and, like the road coaches, they often had names painted on their sides. The first to run on the Liverpool & Manchester Railway were called 'The

*3rd class 1840*

Times', 'Experience', 'The Traveller'
and 'The Victory'. The passengers'
luggage was piled on the roof of the
carriage and although it was covered
up with a sheet it sometimes got
damaged by sparks from the engine.
'Travelling porters', as they were
called, sat on little seats level with
the roof tops. Their job was to keep
an eye on the luggage and the safety
of the train and to help with the
luggage at the stations. It cannot
have been a nice job. Just imagine

*2nd class 1839*

sitting on the roof of a train in all weathers!

These first class carriages had cushioned seats, but there was very little room in them compared with modern carriages, and there was no form of heating in winter and no light at night. In winter, passengers wrapped themselves up in rugs and took special little travelling candle-lamps with them which they lit when it got dark.

The second class carriages had

hard wooden seats, a roof and wooden sides, but there were no windows between these sides and the roof; they were just open to the weather.

The third class carriages did not even have a roof. They were simply open trucks in which the passengers had to stand or, if they were lucky, sit on simple plank seats without any back-rests.

All these first railway carriages ran on four wheels, but very soon longer carriages running on six wheels began to be built, and these ran more smoothly. First class carriages became more roomy and comfortable and looked less like road coaches. Passengers were given footwarmers in winter which looked like big metal hot-water bottles.

At night, each compartment had a single oil lamp in the roof. When it got dark the train would stop at a station where these lamps were waiting ready lit on the platform. The porters would

then run along the roofs of the carriages dropping the lamps into the holders made for them.

The second and third class passengers were not so lucky. They were given no footwarmers or lamps and they still sat on hard wooden seats. For many years the railway companies went on making very uncomfortable second and third class carriages because they thought that by doing so they would force passengers to buy the more expensive first class tickets. But this only meant that people who had not got a lot of money would not travel by train at all if they could possibly help it.

The first company to make third class carriages with comfortable cushioned seats was the old Midland Railway. All the other railways were horrified and said they would be ruined, but of course the Midland Railway was right. Many more people began to travel regularly by their trains and the other railways soon had to improve their carriages too.

The Midland Railway were also the first to use long carriages which ran on two four-wheeled trucks, or 'bogies' as they are called, like all railway carriages do today.

This was in 1874, but even then these new long coaches still had no corridors or connections between one coach and the next. A passenger could not move from his compartment while the train was going along. Because of this even the fastest trains had to stop fairly often so that the passengers could get out, have something to eat in the station refreshment room and use the station lavatories.

For many years all the trains on the main line of the Great Western Railway used to stop for refreshments at Swindon, and the trains leaving Euston would stop at Wolverton for the same reason.

Although special restaurant carriages and sleeping cars were put into service for first class passengers in the 1870s, people had to stay in them during the whole journey because there was no means of passing from one carriage to another while the train was moving. The Great Western Railway put an end to this difficulty in 1892 when they built the first corridor train with flexible connections between the carriages which made it possible to walk from one to another.

The first improvement on the old oil lamps in trains was gas lighting, but this was dangerous because if there was an accident the gas might catch fire or explode. So today all our trains are brightly lit by electricity which the train makes as it goes along.

Every carriage, too, is heated by steam which is supplied by the engine so there is no need for us to wrap ourselves up in rugs like our great-grandfathers did. They had been used to travelling by road coach, sometimes on an outside seat in rain or snow, so they thought the first railway trains were a wonderful improvement. I wonder what they would think of our modern express trains which are really like travelling hotels with everything that the passenger needs for his comfort carried on board.

# Signals and Safety

O NE of the first things you notice on a railway, especially near the stations, are the signals. Those with red or yellow arms on tall white posts are called semaphore signals. If these arms hang down or incline upwards they tell the driver of a train that the line is clear ahead. But if one of the red signal arms stands at right-angles to the signal post it means 'danger' and the driver must stop at once.

The yellow arms are called 'distant' signals and when they are in the horizontal position they say to the driver: 'Go very carefully because you may find the next red signal at danger'. Obviously if the driver of a train was going very fast and he suddenly came to a stop signal at danger he could not pull up at once, so the distant signal is there to warn him to slow down.

On the earliest railways there were no signals at all. The first railway signalmen were called policemen. They stood beside the line and signalled to the driver by moving their arms in different ways or by waving red or green flags. When the first signals were built the signalmen stood beside them to work them. The points, too, which turn a train from one line on to another, had to be worked by levers close beside them.

Stop          Caution

As stations got bigger and busier, this old arrangement could not work any longer. Too many signalmen and pointsmen were needed and if only one of these men made a mistake there could be a bad accident.

So all the signals and points were connected by long wires and rods to a row of levers fixed in a little house called a signal box which was built close beside the railway. Here all the points and signals could be worked by one or two signalmen.

To make this arrangement safer still the signal and point levers were connected in such a way that the signalman could not make a mistake by signalling the driver to go one way but setting the points for his train to go another way.

Very soon after the first railways were built, two men named Cooke and Wheatstone invented the electric telegraph and this was soon used to make the railways safer. Signalmen at different stations could not talk to each other on the telephone as they can today, but they could signal to each other in code by means of the telegraph.

Signalmen still use a special code of bell signals to advise each other about the trains. If you stand near a busy signal box you may hear these bells ringing. They not only warn the signalman to expect a train but they tell him what kind of train it is.

This is the sort of thing that happens all day long in a busy signal box. A bell rings once which means that the signalman in the box next down the line is calling 'Are you there?' Our signalman says 'Yes' by giving one ring back. Then the bell rings four times which means 'Can you accept an express passenger train into your section of the line?' If the line is clear our signalman gives four rings on the bell in reply. The next signal he hears and replies to is two beats on the bell which means: 'The train is just passing my signal box and coming into your section.' Now the signals will be showing 'all clear' for the express and as it roars past the signal box our signalman will throw his signal levers back to danger and ring back to his friend down the line two rings, pause, one ring which means: 'The train has passed my box and is out of the section.'

Our signalman is a very busy man because he has got to make the same bell signals to the next signalman along the line so that he in turn can accept the train from him. He also has to move the needles of little electric machines called 'block instruments' which make absolutely certain that there shall be only one train on one section of the line at a time. Otherwise a fast train could easily run into the back of a slower one.

This system is very reliable, but it is also very expensive because between

each section there must be a signal
box, manned by a signalman day and
night. On very busy lines it is particularly expensive because the sections
have to be very short to allow as many
trains as possible to pass. So it is that
on up-to-date 'inter-city' main lines
the old system has been replaced by
modern methods of electric signalling.
On these lines, hundreds of wayside
signal boxes have been closed. In their
place are a few large signal boxes

which control the signals and points electrically over many miles of line. The men who work in these modern signal boxes may never see the trains they are controlling. Instead they watch an illuminated map of the railway on which little lights come on to show them where the trains are.

You can tell at once where this new system is in use because the old semaphore signals have been replaced by modern, powerful electric colour-light signals. Showing red, yellow and green, they give the driver the same messages, but they are safer because they are more easily seen in darkness or fog. Such signals may be worked by the trains themselves by a system called 'continuous track circuiting'. This works by passing an electric current through the rails so that a passing train completes the circuit and changes the signals. But the object of such modern systems is exactly the same as the old. It is to prevent two trains from ever being on one section of line at the same time. This is called the 'absolute block system'.

We have been talking so far about busy railways where there are two or even four lines, and where trains on any one of these lines always travel in the same direction. On many country branch railways there is only one line of rails so that trains travelling in opposite directions could meet head-on unless special care was taken.

The driver of a train entering a stretch of single line carries with him a 'staff' or a 'ticket'. This is given to him by the signalman at one end of the single line and is his permission to go on. Once he has got it, no other train can move on that bit of line until he has handed it in to the signalman at the other end.

This system, too, can now be operated electrically in much the same way as main lines are now controlled.

Electric operation is so much more
efficient that on some railways which
were originally double track it has
now been possible to take up one of the

tracks. With only one line to look after, this means that a lot of money is saved.

Another thing which has made railway travelling much safer since the early days is a better form of brake. The old trains only had brakes on the engine tender and on the guard's van which were screwed on by hand.

All British passenger trains now use what is called the vacuum brake, which acts on every wheel of the train. Between each pair of coaches you will see two pipes. One of these is for the steam heating and the other is the brake pipe. When the train is running there is a vacuum (this means no air) in the pipe and this keeps the brakes off. If they want to stop the train the driver or the guard can open a valve which lets air into the pipe and puts the brake on. An arrangement on the engine called an 'ejector' sucks the air out of the pipe again and releases the brakes when the train is ready to move.

If a coupling between two carriages were to break while a train was going along, the brake pipe would be broken too. The air would at once rush in, put on all the brakes and so stop both halves of the broken train before any accident could happen.

All the many clever things which engineers have invented to make railway travelling so safe act in the same way as this vacuum brake by always doing the 'safe' thing if anything goes wrong. If a signal wire breaks, the signal flies to danger at once. In the same way all the complicated electrical signalling arrangements which are used on modern railways give a danger signal if the electric current fails.

# Railway engines of today

IN 1960 there were 16,000 steam loco-motives at work on British Rail-ways, but it had already been decided that steam must go and in August, 1968, the last of them, named 'Oliver Cromwell', made its farewell run. Today you can only see steam loco-motives in museums or on the few short railways where they have been kept at work by railway lovers.

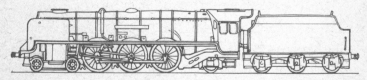

*Stanier Pacific*

Throughout British Railways, diesel power has taken the place of steam on all lines that have not been electrified. Because diesel engines have been used for so many years in buses and lorries on our roads, you may wonder why this change has not come about sooner on our railways. The main reason is this. Steam power is so flexible that on a steam locomotive its wheels can be driven directly from the pistons by rods and cranks. In order to produce its power, a diesel engine has to run at a much higher speed than the travelling wheels so that some form of gearing is needed between the two. In the case of a diesel lorry or bus on the road, a clutch and a gearbox similar to those fitted to our cars are used to transmit the power of the engine to the wheels. But on a railway locomotive which has to be able to move a very heavy train from a standstill and then pick up speed smoothly to 80 or 90 miles an hour something much

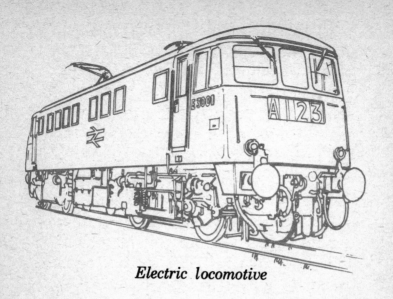

*Electric locomotive*

more complicated and expensive is needed.

Most of the locomotives that now pull our trains are known as 'diesel-electrics'. The diesel engine drives a dynamo which supplies current to electric motors which turn the driving wheels. They are simply electric locomotives which make their own electricity. Locomotives of this kind are much more expensive to build than the older steam engines. On the other hand, they spend less time standing in the engine shed because they need

*The driver's cabin — old and new style*

less looking after. Also, they can pull heavy goods trains just as easily as expresses whereas, in steam days, a special kind of engine with small driving wheels was needed for goods trains. For both these reasons, far fewer diesel locomotives are now needed to work the trains on our railways than was the case in the days of steam.

These modern diesel locomotives may not look so exciting as the steam locomotives with their moving rods and great driving wheels, but they make life very much easier for the men who have to work them. Standing in the open, draughty cab of a steam locomotive in all weathers was no joke, while on a long run the fireman had to shovel many tons of coal into the firebox to keep up the steam. Now both men can sit comfortably in a closed cab, looking out through a windscreen. And because this cab is right in front of the engine instead of behind a great long boiler, they get a much better view of the line ahead and the signals than they used to do in the old days.

Stopping passenger trains on short runs used to be drawn by special small steam locomotives called suburban tank engines. Now such trains look as if they had no engines at all. Railway-men call them D.M.U.s (Diesel Multiple Units). They are driven by

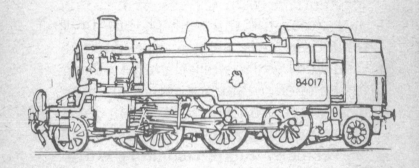

diesel engines under the carriage floors and, because their weight is small, these engines drive the wheels through an automatic gear-box such as is used in some road vehicles. They are arranged so that two or more short trains can be coupled together and driven by one man who sits in a cab in the front of the first carriage. This is why they are called 'Multiple Units'.

Electric railways are much older in origin than the diesel engine. As long ago as 1910 there were 200 miles of electric railway in England, a total which does not include underground railways like those in London. Electricity is an almost ideal power for railways. Its only drawback is that it is so expensive to install. Because of its high cost, the first railways to be electrified were those near London which carried a great many suburban passenger trains making frequent stops. These lines have now become part of the Southern Region of British Railways. Since the early days this electrification has spread so that electric trains now run to Portsmouth, Southampton, Brighton and to many towns in Kent.

All these Southern Region trains, like the trains on London's Under-

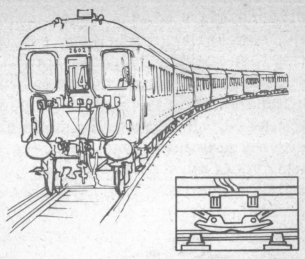

Side view of the collecting
shoe of an electric train

ground, pick up their electric power
by means of a metal shoe which
presses on a third rail laid alongside
the two rails on which they run. They
are driven by electric motors built
into the carriage bogies. So, like the
D.M.U.'s mentioned earlier, the trains
look as if they had no engine pulling
them, while a number of short trains
can be coupled together and driven by
one man.

The busiest main line in Britain (and one of the first to be built) is the one running from London (Euston) to Birmingham, Crewe, Liverpool and Manchester. Because traffic on this railway was so heavy, British Railways decided to electrify it as part of their plan to bring Britain's railways up to date. Instead of using a third rail, the trains on this line pick up their electric power from a single wire overhead in the same way that the old street tramcars used to do. This is much less dangerous to men who have to work on the line. The overhead wire also makes it possible to use electricity at much higher pressure (voltage) and this is more economical.

Stopping trains on this new electric railway look very much the same as those on the Southern Region except for the arrangement on the roof (called a 'pantagraph') which picks up the electricity from the wire. But all the expresses and the goods trains are drawn by electric locomotives. Because they do not need to carry diesel engines to generate the power which drives them, these electric engines look very small and neat. But they are tremendously powerful and can haul the heaviest express trains at speeds of more than 100 miles an hour. Such speeds are necessary now that railways have to compete with the motor car and the aeroplane.

# A railway journey

WHEN you know something about railways and their history you will find a railway journey much more interesting. There is always plenty to look at. Let us imagine we are off to the seaside from one of the big London stations. There, waiting at the platform, stands our express train with a blue diesel locomotive, long and powerful looking, at the head of it. As well as a number, it may carry a name on its side like express

steam locomotives used to do.

Soon after we have taken our seats the signal at the end of the platform changes from red to green and our guard blows his whistle and waves his green flag as a signal to start. Our locomotive gives a toot on its horn in acknowledgement, its engine roars and we begin to move. We go slowly at first until we get clear of all the points, sidings and buildings. Then, as we head for open country, we rapidly pick up speed until we are travelling at seventy, eighty or even ninety miles an hour. We flash through wayside stations with a tremendous roar and so fast that we may not have time to read their names. Perhaps we overtake a goods train rumbling steadily along on another line.

There are lots of little things to notice beside the line if the train is not going too fast.

Every quarter of a mile there is a

post which tells us how far we have travelled. There are other posts which tell us whether the line is rising or falling. '1 in 150' such a post may say, which means that the line climbs one foot for every 150 feet we travel forward.

If the train suddenly slows down but is not coming into any station it means one of two things. Either a signal is showing 'caution' because the line ahead is not clear or else all the trains are being slowed down because repair work of some kind is

Continuously welded rails being laid in position from a specially equipped train

going on.

Perhaps a bridge is being rebuilt or new rails are being laid down. Drivers are usually warned about such work beforehand and know when they must slow down, but if anything goes wrong on the line unexpectedly they can be warned by one of the workmen who puts a signal called a detonator on the line which makes a loud bang when the engine wheel hits it.

'Diddle-di-dum, Diddle-di-dum' sing the wheels of our carriage as they run over the rail joints and although we ride along so smoothly, in fact each joint gives the rim of the wheel a blow like a hammer. The force of this blow could be so great that it cracked the steel tyres of the wheels or broke the rails near the joints. So these joints are rapidly being replaced now by rails that have been welded together at the ends to make very long continuous lengths. We can tell as soon as our train passes on to this new kind of track because the familiar 'Diddle-di-dum' noise of the wheels stops at once and all we can hear is a steady roaring noise.

This new kind of rail is usually laid on concrete sleepers in place of the older wooden ones. If you look out of the window and watch the other line, you may be able to spot these new concrete sleepers because they are lighter in colour.

If our train is taking us into the West Country or to Wales, the country gets more hilly as we near the end of our journey. Our train thunders over high viaducts or through long tunnels. The tunnels are usually at the top of long gradients. You will notice that the railway always climbs up the side of the valley of some river until it becomes a tiny stream and it can follow it no longer. This is where the railway engineers were compelled to tunnel through the hills to the head of another valley on the other side.

In such hilly country we can tell that our engine is having to work very hard. In the days of steam locomotives, even express trains used to stop at the bottom of some particularly steep inclines so that a second engine could run out of a siding and help to push the train over the hill. Railwaymen called this 'banking', but because modern diesel locomotives are much more powerful, 'banking' engines are very seldom needed today.

We have climbed the last of these hills now and as we are running down from the tunnel or the deep cutting at the top, suddenly the blue sea comes into sight.

We have come to the end of our long journey. Very soon our train has stopped at the platform of the seaside terminus and the waiting porters are opening the carriage doors.

If we had made such a journey only a few years ago we should have been drawn by a steam locomotive. Its tender, piled high with coal at the start, would be nearly empty now, for the fireman would have had to shovel as much as eight tons on to the fire. And when a steam locomotive had finished such a long journey it had to go to the engine shed to have its fire cleaned and remade, the boiler tubes and smoke-box cleared of soot, all the moving parts inspected and oiled, and the tender refilled with coal and water before it was ready for the return journey.

But our diesel locomotive stands at the platform with its enginemen looking as clean and fresh as they did when we started our journey. Their engine only needs to be filled up with fuel oil before it is ready for the long run back to London.

For us this long journey has been an exciting adventure which only happens perhaps once or twice a year. But remember that the train we have just left, like thousands of others, makes the same long journey every weekday, summer and winter in every kind of weather, year after year. At this very moment hundreds of trains of every kind from great Scottish expresses to little local trains on country branch lines are on the move. Yet how very, very seldom do we hear of any bad railway accident. Railways are in fact the safest way of travelling that has ever been invented.

For this we have to thank the cleverness of the railway engineers and the care of all the men who work on the railways.

It was not only the driver and the guard of our train who brought us so safely and quickly from London to the seaside, but also a lot of men we did not see; men in the engine shed who made our engine ready for its run; men who had walked over every mile of the railway to make sure the track was safe and sound; men in lonely signal boxes whose signals and messages protected us from start to stop. Day and night their work goes on, for perhaps the most wonderful thing about railways is that they never stop. Always the trains are on the move. They have been carrying goods and passengers every day since the first train ran from Liverpool to Manchester much more than one hundred years ago.

# SOME BOOKS TO READ

**THE STUDY BOOK OF RAILWAYS**
Eric Baxter, Bodley Head, 1964

**TUBE TRAINS UNDER LONDON**
J. G. Bruce, London Transport, 1968

**LOCOMOTIVES**
D. C. Joiner, Wills and Hepworth, 1964

**RAILWAYS**
J. S. Murphy, Oxford University Press, 1964

**THE STORY OF BRITISH LOCOMOTIVES**
B. W. Way, Methuen, 1964

**RAILWAYS**
Boswell Taylor, Brockhampton, 1967

# Index